Put Beginning Readers on the Right Track with
ALL ABOARD READING™

The All Aboard Reading series is especially designed for beginning readers. Written by noted authors and illustrated in full color, these are books that children really want to read—books to excite their imagination, expand their interests, make them laugh, and support their feelings. With fiction and nonfiction stories that are high interest and curriculum-related, All Aboard Reading books offer something for every young reader. And with four different reading levels, the All Aboard Reading series lets you choose which books are most appropriate for your children and their growing abilities.

Picture Readers
Picture Readers have super-simple texts, with many nouns appearing as rebus pictures. At the end of each book are 24 flash cards—on one side is a rebus picture; on the other side is the written-out word.

Station Stop 1
Station Stop 1 books are best for children who have just begun to read. Simple words and big type make these early reading experiences more comfortable. Picture clues help children to figure out the words on the page. Lots of repetition throughout the text helps children to predict the next word or phrase—an essential step in developing word recognition.

Station Stop 2
Station Stop 2 books are written specifically for children who are reading with help. Short sentences make it easier for early readers to understand what they are reading. Simple plots and simple dialogue help children with reading comprehension.

Station Stop 3
Station Stop 3 books are perfect for children who are reading alone. With longer text and harder words, these books appeal to children who have mastered basic reading skills. More complex stories captivate children who are ready for more challenging books.

In addition to All Aboard Reading books, look for All Aboard Math Readers™ (fiction stories that teach math concepts children are learning in school); All Aboard Science Readers™ (nonfiction books that explore the most fascinating science topics in age-appropriate language); All Aboard Poetry Readers™ (funny, rhyming poems for readers of all levels); and All Aboard Mystery Readers™ (puzzling tales where children piece together evidence with the characters).

All Aboard for happy reading!

For Jay, who tolerates my elephant obsession,
and for Dylan, who loves elephants, too,
and does an excellent trumpeting call!—G.L.C.

To my Mom, with love.—R.C.

GROSSET & DUNLAP
Published by the Penguin Group
Penguin Group (USA) Inc., 375 Hudson Street, New York, New York 10014, USA
Penguin Group (Canada), 90 Eglinton Avenue East, Suite 700, Toronto,
Ontario M4P 2Y3, Canada
(a division of Pearson Penguin Canada Inc.)
Penguin Books Ltd., 80 Strand, London WC2R 0RL, England
Penguin Group Ireland, 25 St. Stephen's Green, Dublin 2, Ireland
(a division of Penguin Books Ltd.)
Penguin Group (Australia), 250 Camberwell Road, Camberwell, Victoria 3124, Australia
(a division of Pearson Australia Group Pty. Ltd.)
Penguin Books India Pvt. Ltd., 11 Community Centre, Panchsheel Park,
New Delhi—110 017, India
Penguin Group (NZ), 67 Apollo Drive, Rosedale, North Shore 0632, New Zealand
(a division of Pearson New Zealand Ltd.)
Penguin Books (South Africa) (Pty.) Ltd., 24 Sturdee Avenue,
Rosebank, Johannesburg 2196, South Africa

Penguin Books Ltd., Registered Offices:
80 Strand, London WC2R 0RL, England

Text copyright © 2009 by Ginjer L. Clarke. Illustrations copyright © 2009 by Robbin Cuddy. All
rights reserved. Published by Grosset & Dunlap, a division of Penguin Young Readers Group,
345 Hudson Street, New York, New York 10014. ALL ABOARD READING and GROSSET &
DUNLAP are trademarks of Penguin Group (USA) Inc. Printed in the U.S.A.

Library of Congress Cataloging-in-Publication Data

Clarke, Ginjer L.
Baby elephant / by Ginjer L. Clarke ; illustrations by Robbin Cuddy.
p. cm. -- (All aboard science reader. Station stop 2)
ISBN 978-0-448-44825-1 (pbk.)
1. Elephants--Infancy--Juvenile literature. I. Cuddy, Robbin, ill. II. Title.
QL737.P98C57 2009
599.67'139--dc22
2008020696

ISBN 978-0-448-44825-1   10 9 8 7 6 5 4 3 2 1

Baby Elephant

By Ginjer L. Clarke
Illustrated by Robbin Cuddy

Grosset & Dunlap

Nighttime is coming
on the African grassland.
An elephant family lies down
under a group of trees.
They usually sleep for
only two or three hours at a time.

But they will rest longer tonight.

One of the young female elephants

is having her first baby.

An elephant baby grows inside
its mother for almost two years.
When it is born, the baby elephant
weighs 200 pounds and is three feet tall.
That is more than 20 times heavier
than a human baby!

The baby elephant has black fuzz
on her forehead and back.

This hair will fall out as she gets older.

Her skin is dry and scratchy.

She can get a sunburn, just like you.

The baby elephant sucks her short trunk, just like a human baby sucks its thumb. She will be almost one year old before she learns to use her trunk to eat.

For now, she curls her trunk over her head
and drinks her mother's milk.
The mother elephant uses her trunk
to hug her new baby.

Whoops!

The baby elephant is wobbly at first.

But she can walk in less than an hour!

She has to learn to walk quickly.

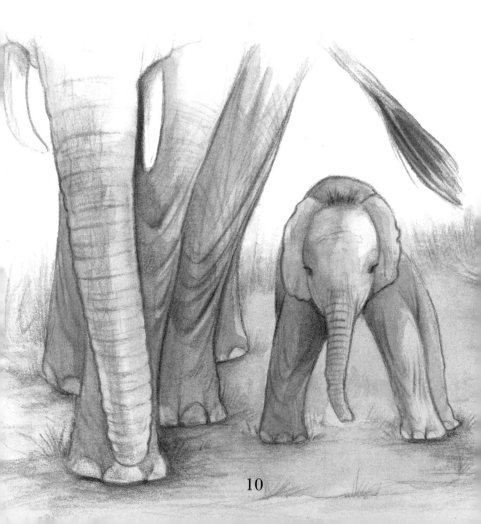

Elephant families do not stay
in one place for very long.

They are always looking for food and water.

And they keep away from animals like lions
that could hurt the baby elephant.

After the baby has had enough time to rest,

the new mother and baby are ready to go.

All of the elephants touch and smell

the new baby to welcome her.

The elephant family forms a line.

They walk all night long.

They are looking for water.

Younger elephants hold their mothers' tails
so they do not get lost or left behind.

The new baby walks under her mother.
She is safe with her family.

It is almost morning now.

The elephants are very thirsty.

They call to one another in low rumbles

so they can keep together.

They even make sounds that

people cannot hear.

Ha-rooo!

One elephant at the front of the line trumpets loudly with her trunk.

She has found a water hole!

Splash!

The elephants swim in the water
and roll in the mud.

Elephants get a lot of bug bites.

The mud stops them from itching.

The baby elephant can swim almost as soon as she can walk. And she can even drink her mother's milk underwater!

A trunk is like an elephant's nose and lips.

The baby elephant sucks up water

with her trunk like a straw.

She pours the water into her mouth.

Adult elephants can drink

up to 60 gallons a day.

A trunk is also used like your hands.

It even has two small "fingers" on the end.

The fingers help elephants pick up things.

Elephants use their trunks to smell, talk,

touch, kiss, drink, eat, and shower.

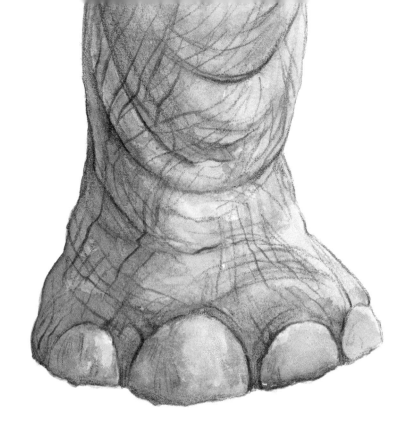

Elephant feet are not like your feet.

African elephants have four toes

on their front feet,

and three toes on their back feet.

But elephants walk on their tiptoes,

because of the way their foot bones

are shaped.

And they can walk very quietly,

because their feet are soft and padded.

It is easy to spot elephant tracks.

An elephant's big, round footprint

is about the size of a car tire!

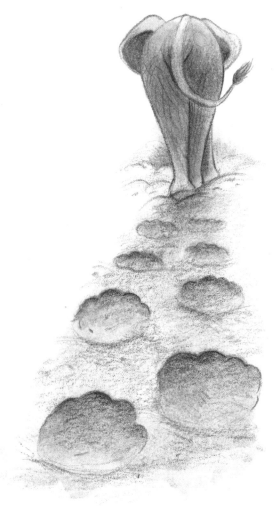

It is time for a snack.

Crrr-ack!

The mother elephant breaks off
the branches of a prickly tree.
She uses her big teeth to chew.
Elephants can grow new teeth when
the old ones get worn out from chewing.

Elephants do not eat meat.

They like to eat grass, leaves, and bamboo.

They also like to eat fruit like figs,

coconuts, and bananas.

Elephants eat a lot—

up to 440 pounds of food each day!

When the baby elephant grows up,

she will weigh as much as four tons.

Adult elephants stand about ten feet tall.

That is higher than most ceilings.

Elephants are the heaviest land animals.

The only animals bigger are whales.

The only animals taller are giraffes.

Elephants are enormous!

African elephant ears can be
up to five feet wide.
Elephants flap their huge ears
like fans to keep themselves cool.
They say things with their ears, too.
An angry elephant sticks her ears way out.

A sad elephant lays her ears back flat.

Elephant ears are like people's fingerprints.

They have different shapes, spots, and sizes.

No two ears are exactly the same!

Male African elephants are
much bigger than females.
Males are called bulls.
Females are called cows.
Their babies are called calves.
A family of elephants is made up of
adult females and their calves.

This group is called a herd.

Male elephants leave the herd

when they are about thirteen years old.

They sometimes travel with older males.

But they mostly live on their own.

Both male and female elephants
have tusks made of ivory.
Ivory is hard, like your teeth.
These tusks start to grow when
elephants are two years old.
Tusks can be used like tools
to dig in the dirt for food.

The tusks of males are much longer
than the ones female elephants have.
Males use their tusks to fight.
These pointed weapons are dangerous!

Sometimes humans kill African elephants

for their beautiful ivory tusks.

The ivory is used to make jewelry,

buttons, piano keys, and other things.

African elephants are

protected by laws in most places.

But people still kill elephants

because they fear them,

and for their tusks.

These elephants are usually gentle
and stay away from people.
But sometimes the elephants
wander into villages and farms.
It is hard for them to find space to live in,
because people live in the areas
where the elephants used to roam free.

Elephants have been around

for a long time.

They are related to the mammoths.

Some mammoths were still alive

8,000 years ago,

but they are all extinct now.

Some were woolly, but some were not.

Many mammoths were not as big

as African elephants.

Some of them had long tusks

that curled around!

Less than 30 years ago, there were more than 1 million African elephants. Now, only about half of them are left.

But some parks in Africa are helping
to keep these elephants safe.
And many baby elephants have been born
in zoos around the world.
So we hope they will be around
for a long time to come!

African elephants have smaller cousins
that live in the forests of Asia.
There are only about 40,000
Asian elephants left in the wild.

They are running out of forests to live in.

Farmers get angry when elephants

eat their trees and crops.

But the elephants are just hungry.

You can tell African and Asian elephants
apart by the shapes of their ears.
African elephant ears are bigger
and look like a map of Africa.
Asian elephant ears are smaller
and look like a map of Asia.

Asian elephants have only one finger

on their trunks instead of two.

All African elephants have tusks,

but female Asian elephants do not.

These cousins look a lot alike,

but they have very different lives.

Most African elephants live in the wild.

Some Asian elephants have jobs

that people make them do.

People use them to carry logs, to ride on,

to push wagons, and to lift heavy objects.

They were used in wars long ago.

Asian elephants are trained for the circus.

Sometimes they are painted and dressed up

for special celebrations.

These elephants are very special to

the Hindu people of India.

An elephant family is very close.

The oldest female leads the herd.

She is called the *matriarch*.

(You say it like this: MAY-tree-ark.)

She is 50 years old!

She shows her sisters and daughters

and all of their babies

where to find food and water.

She teaches her family
everything they need to know.
What a great grandmother!

Elephants are very smart.

They remember things for a long time.

That is why some people say that

"an elephant never forgets."

Elephants get sad when one of

their family members is sick or dies.

Some scientists believe that

elephants can even cry.

Elephants also show that
they care about one another.
They hug and kiss with their trunks.
Female elephants protect one another
and take good care of their babies.

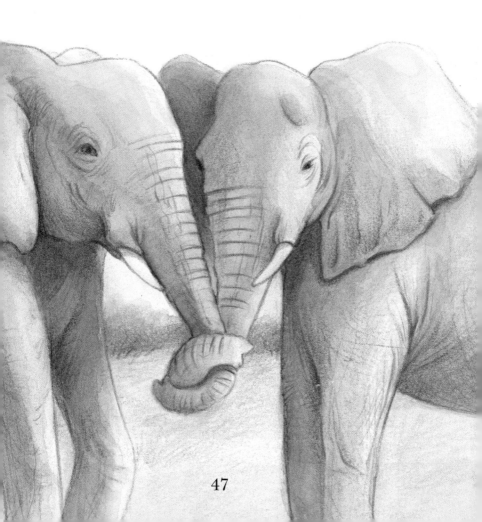

This baby elephant is big and beautiful.

Her mother watches over her,

just like your mother loves you.

People and elephants do not look alike.

But we do many things in the same way.

Baby elephants are a lot like you!